BRITISH RAILWAYS STEAMING THROUGH WALES AND THE WELSH BORDER

Compiled by
PETER HANDS

DEFIANT PUBLICATIONS
190 Yoxall Road,
Shirley, Solihull,
West Midlands

Printed on behalf of Richard Netherwood Ltd., by Gorenjski tisk p.o. Slovenia.

CURRENT STEAM PHOTOGRAPH ALBUMS AVAILABLE FROM DEFIANT PUBLICATIONS

VOLUME 14
A4 size - Hardback. 96 pages
-178 b/w photographs.
£14.95 + £1.50 postage.
ISBN 0 946857 40 7.

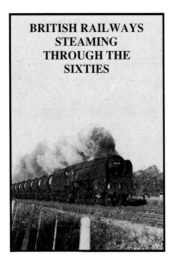

VOLUME 15
A4 size - Hardback. 96 pages
-178 b/w photographs.
£16.95 + £1.50 postage.
ISBN 0 946857 52 0.

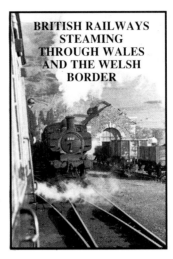

A4 size - Hardback. 96 pages
-175 b/w photographs.
£17.95 + £1.50 postage.
ISBN 0 946857 56 3.

VOLUME 1
A4 size - Hardback. 96 pages
-177 b/w photographs.
£14.95 + £1.50 postage.
ISBN 0 946857 41 5.

VOLUME 9
A4 size - Hardback. 96 pages
-177 b/w photographs.
£14.95 + £1.50 postage.
ISBN 0 946857 37 7.

VOLUME 10
A4 size - Hardback. 96 pages
-176 b/w photographs.
£14.95 + £1.50 postage.
ISBN 0 946857 38 5.

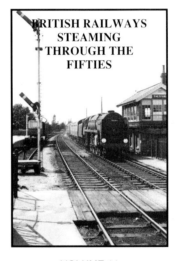

VOLUME 11
A4 size - Hardback. 96 pages
-176 b/w photographs.
£16.95 + £1.50 postage.
ISBN 0 946857 48 2.

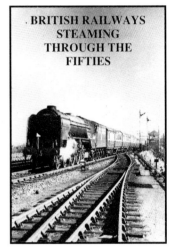

VOLUME 12
A4 size - Hardback. 96 pages
-176 b/w photographs.
£16.95 + £1.50 postage.
ISBN 0 946857 49 0.

VOLUME 1
A4 size - Hardback. 96 pages
-177 b/w photographs.
£14.95 + £1.50 postage.
ISBN 0 946857 39 3.

VOLUME 1
A4 size - Hardback. 96 pages
-174 b/w photographs.
£14.95 + £1.50 postage.
ISBN 0 946857 42 3.

VOLUME 1
A4 size - Hardback. 96 pages
-179 b/w photographs.
£15.95 + £1.50 postage.
ISBN 0 946857 43 I.

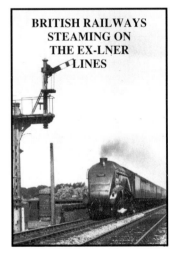

VOLUME 3
A4 size - Hardback. 96 pages
-183 b/w photographs.
£15.95 + £1.50 postage.
ISBN 0 946857 44 X.

FUTURE STEAM PHOTOGRAPH ALBUMS
AND OTHER TITLES

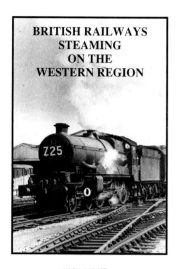

BRITISH RAILWAYS STEAMING ON THE WESTERN REGION

VOLUME 4
A4 size - Hardback. 96 pages
-177 b/w photographs.
£15.95 + £1.50 postage.
ISBN 0 946857 46 6.

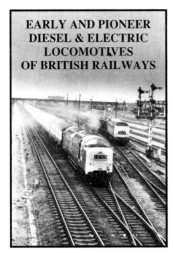

EARLY AND PIONEER DIESEL & ELECTRIC LOCOMOTIVES OF BRITISH RAILWAYS

A4 size - Hardback. 96 pages
-177 b/w photographs.
£15.95 + £1.50 postage.
ISBN 0 946857 45 8.

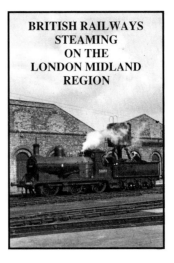

BRITISH RAILWAYS STEAMING ON THE LONDON MIDLAND REGION

VOLUME 4
A4 size - Hardback. 96 pages
-177 b/w photographs.
£15.95 + £1.50 postage.
ISBN 0 946857 47 4.

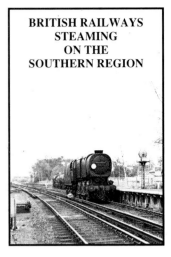

BRITISH RAILWAYS STEAMING ON THE SOUTHERN REGION

VOLUME 3
A4 size - Hardback. 96 pages
-177 b/w photographs.
£17.95 + £1.50 postage.
ISBN 0 946857 54 7.

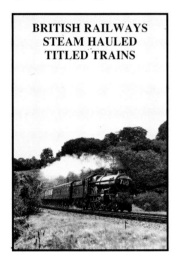

BRITISH RAILWAYS STEAM HAULED TITLED TRAINS

A4 size - Hardback. 96 pages
-169 b/w photographs.
£16.95 + £1.50 postage.
ISBN 0 946857 51 2.

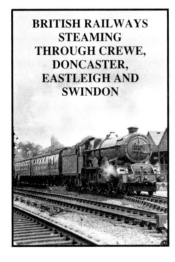

BRITISH RAILWAYS STEAMING THROUGH CREWE, DONCASTER, EASTLEIGH AND SWINDON

A4 size - Hardback. 96 pages
-179 b/w photographs.
£17.95 + £1.50 postage.
ISBN 0 946857 53 9.

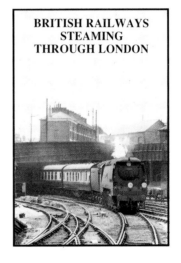

BRITISH RAILWAYS STEAMING THROUGH LONDON

A4 size - Hardback. 96 pages
-174 b/w photographs.
£17.95 + £1.50 postage.
ISBN 0 946857 55 5.

BRITISH RAILWAYS STEAMING ON THE EX-LNER LINES

VOLUME 4
A4 size - Hardback. 96 pages
-183 b/w photographs.
£17.95 + £1.50 postage.
ISBN 0 946857 57 1.

BRITISH RAILWAYS STEAMING FROM 1948–1968

'50th' ALBUM
A4 size - Hardback. 96 pages
-186 b/w photographs.
£16.95 + £1.50 postage.
ISBN 0 946857 50 4.

BRITISH RAILWAYS STEAMING ON THE LONDON MIDLAND REGION

IN PREPARATION

VOLUME 5

BRITISH RAILWAYS STEAMING ON THE WESTERN REGION

IN PREPARATION

VOLUME 5

It's a dog's life in the FIRE SERVICE
by Peter St.Bernard

COMEDY
269 pages. Cartoons.
£9.95 + £1.00 postage.
ISBN 0 946857 30 X.

ACKNOWLEDGEMENTS

Grateful thanks are extended to the following contributors of photographs not only for their use in this book but for their kind patience and long term loan of negatives/photographs whilst this book was being compiled.

T.R.AMOS TAMWORTH	BRIAN BENNETT BURGESS HILL	H.H.BLEADS BIRMINGHAM
B.W.L.BROOKSBANK MORDEN	N.L.BROWNE ALDERSHOT	L.BROWNHILL PENHOSS
R.BUTTERFIELD MIRFIELD	R.S.CARPENTER BIRMINGHAM	TIM FAREBROTHER BOURTON
A.N.H.GLOVER BIRMINGHAM	B.K.B.GREEN WARRINGTON	D.HARRISON CHAPELTOWN
PETER HAY HOVE	R.W.HINTON GLOUCESTER	H.L.HOLLAND ST.CATHERINES, ONTARIO, CANADA
F.HORNBY NORTH CHEAM	A.C.INGRAM WISBECH	D.I.JOHN LLANSAMLET
D.K.JONES MOUNTAIN ASH	T.LEWIS *	DENIS LEWIS TEIGNMOUTH
T.B.OWEN CAEMELYN	S.L.C.PHILIPS LLANDYSSUL	R.PICTON WOLVERHAMPTON
W.POTTER BISHOPS CLEEVE	N.E.PREEDY GLOUCESTER	J.SCHATZ LITTLETHORPE
M.S.STOKES MARPLE	J.M.TOLSON BIGGLESWADE	KIT WINDLE LOWER BREDBURY

* Courtesy of the Norman Preedy collection

Front Cover - GWR 5700 Class 0-6-0PT No 7717, from 88D Merthyr, is seen high in the Welsh hills at Talybont-on-Usk with a passenger train on 27th October 1955. Once of Brecon and Merthyr Tydfil Railway origin, the station at Talybont-on-Usk closed for good during 1962. No 7717 was transferred later in the fifties to 88A Cardiff (Radyr) and 88C Barry, being withdrawn from the latter in March 1960. (N.E.Preedy)

ISBN 0 946857 56 3

© PETER HANDS 1996
FIRST PUBLISHED 1996

INTRODUCTION

BRITISH RAILWAYS STEAMING THROUGH WALES AND THE WELSH BORDER adds a further dimension to the wide variety of 'BR Steaming' albums published over the years by 'Defiant Publications'.

This album encompasses the work of some thirty contributors and covers well in excess of sixty locations within the Principality of Wales and border towns from the early days of British Railways until the mid-sixties. The author has attempted to vary the locations as much as possible, but some areas of greater interest e.g. Cardiff, Chester and Swansea etc., have been given more coverage than others.

The 'BR Steaming' books are designed to give the ordinary, everyday steam photographic enthusiast of the 1950's and 1960's a chance to participate in and give pleasure to others whilst recapturing the twilight days of steam.

Apart from the 1950's and 1960's series, individual albums like this one will be produced from time to time. Wherever possible, no famous names will be found nor will photographs which have been published before be used. Nevertheless, the content and quality of the majority of photographs used will be second to none.

The majority of the photographs in this album have been contributed by readers of Peter Hands series of booklets entitled "What Happened to Steam" & "BR Steam Shed Allocations" and from readers of the earlier "BR Steaming Through The Sixties" albums. In normal circumstances these may have been hidden from the public eye for ever.

The continuation of the "BR Steaming" series etc., depends upon you the reader. If you wish to join my mailing list for future albums and/or feel you have suitable material of BR steam locomotives between 1948-1968 and wish to contribute them towards this series and other albums, please contact:

Tel. No.
0121 745-8421

Peter Hands,
190 Yoxall Road,
Shirley, Solihull,
West Midlands B90 3RN

CONTENTS

MEMORIES OF WALES AND THE WELSH BORDER

1) Lydney Junction station (Severn & Wye Joint Railway) - July 1950. (R.S.Carpenter)

2) Llangollen Station in April 1967- closed in 1965. (R.W.Hinton)

3) Wrexham North signalbox in April 1967. (R.W.Hinton)

4) Photographed near to the imposing Chester No 6 signalbox, GWR *County* Class 4-6-0 No 1022 *County of Northampton*, from 84G Shrewsbury and equipped with a double chimney in May 1956, turns on the triangle to the west of Chester (General) station on 20th August 1958. *County of Northampton* had been at Shrewsbury shed since a move from 84K Chester three months earlier. It served briefly at 85C Hereford in 1959 before returning to 84G for its final years of service. (M.S.Stokes)

5) GWR P.M. Class 0-4-0ST No 1150 is seen out of steam on a side road at its home shed of 87D Swansea East Dock on 4th May 1952 in the company of 4200 Class 2-8-0T No 5246. No 1150 was one of three such engines which were inherited by the GWR in 1923 from Powlesand and Mason of Swansea to a design by Peckett in 1907. It was withdrawn well before the end of the fifties. Note the Great Western Railway safety valve cover and the warning bell above the cab. (R.W.Hinton)

6) A feather of steam escapes from the safety valve of 86C Cardiff (Canton) based GWR *Castle* Class 4-6-0 No 5005 *Manorbier Castle* as it waits to continue with its journey from Paddington to Cardiff at Newport (High Street) with the down *Capitals United Express* in 1956. Built at Swindon Works in June 1927, *Manorbier Castle* had a brief flirtation in a streamlined condition. It was withdrawn from 82C Swindon in February 1960 after travelling 1,731,868 miles. (R.W.Hinton)

7) Summer foliage is in abundance as two LMS Stanier Class 5 4-6-0's, both with steam to spare, power their way out of Colwyn Bay on the North Wales main line with a nine-coach express on 7th June 1952. Leading the brace is No 44981, allocation not known, which was to serve later in life from the sheds at 21B Bournville, 21A Saltley, 6J Holyhead and 6D Shrewsbury. It was condemned from the latter in January 1967 and cut up at Cashmores, Newport. (T.Lewis)

8) GWR *Castle* Class 4-6-0 No 5037 *Monmouth Castle*, of 85A Worcester, stands on a centre road at Hereford with the stock of a local passenger train on 26th April 1958. Note the straight-sided tender. In June 1960 *Monmouth Castle* was transferred from 85A to 81A Old Oak Common, but just over twelve months later it was drafted to South Wales and had two spells at 87A Neath and 87F Llanelly before moving to a final abode at 82B St.Philip's Marsh. (Denis Lewis)

9) Introduced into traffic in April 1920, GWR Churchward 4200 Class 2-8-0T No 4277 stands in bright sunshine in the yard of its
home shed at 86H Aberbeeg on a summer's day in 1960. Once used on pilot duties through the Severn tunnel between 1948 and
1953, No 4277's main life's work involved moving every kind of mineral ore including iron, coal and steel in South Wales.
Withdrawn in June 1964 it is now a preserved item. (Tim Farebrother)

10) GWR 2251 Class 0-6-0 No 2271 looks in fine fettle as it stands out of steam in front of the two-road repair shop at
87G Carmarthen where it had been based in pre-British Railways days. The six-road shed at Carmarthen was completed on
11th February 1907 and was situated on the north side of the station. It was closed in June 1964 and the surviving steam
locomotives were transferred to 87F Llanelly. No 2271 was withdrawn in September 1962. (B.K.B.Green)

11) As an eastbound express approaches in the distance the footplate crew of GWR 6400 Class 0-6-0PT No 6438, from 88E Abercynon, wait patiently for a clear path to Pontypridd with a local passenger train seen at St.Fagans station, situated between Cardiff and Bridgend on 2nd May 1959. In December 1960 No 6438 was despatched to a new home at 85E Gloucester (Barnwood). Its final home was at 83D Laira (Plymouth) being condemned in November 1962. (S.L.C.Philips)

12) Five months after nationalisation LMS Class 2 2-6-2T No 41204 still bears the logo of its former master as it stands in light steam in the yard of its home base at 4E Tredegar on a wet and miserable 23rd May 1948. Originally owned by the London & North Western Railway, Tredegar became the property of the Western Region in 1955 and was coded 86K from then until complete closure in 1960. No 41204 was destined to survive in service until November 1966. (A.N.H.Glover)

13) The twin roundhouses at 87F Llanelly was a 'treasure trove' of smaller former Great Western Railway locomotives in the early fifties. Nicely captured on film there on 19th April 1953 is ex. Burry Port & Gwendraeth Valley Railway 0-6-0ST No 2176, formerly named *Pembrey*, a product of the Avonmouth Engine Company in 1907. This shed at Llanelly opened in 1925 replacing the 1840 built Llanelly Railway and Dock Company structure. (B.K.B.Green)

14) A rain-swept and dismal looking 8th December 1962 at Hereford station where GWR *Hall* Class 4-6-0 No 5952 *Cogan Hall*, from the local shed at 86C, is employed on a local passenger working. Once of 85A Worcester, *Cogan Hall* had been at Hereford shed since August 1959. In November 1963 it was drafted to pastures new at 88A Cardiff East Dock. After withdrawal in June 1964 it was stored at Barry Docks for many years before being saved for preservation. (J.Schatz)

15) Only a handful of GWR 4-6-0's were ever allocated to the former Port Talbot Railway shed at Duffryn Yard, coded 87B by BR. One of these, *Hall* Class 4-6-0 No 6920 *Barningham Hall*, seen here paired with a straight-sided tender near to the coaling stage, had been transferred to Duffryn Yard a couple of months before this picture was taken in November 1962. It was withdrawn from 87B in December 1963 three months before the shed closed completely. (D.K.Jones)

16) We move the length of Wales to the seaside resort of Llandudno where we find ourselves at the terminus station, of London and North Western Railway origin. On 11th July 1964 two LMS Class 5 4-6-0's are on duty. One, No 45250, from 5A Crewe (North) is in charge of a local passenger train and the other, No 45182, of 9H Patricroft, heads the 4.40pm express bound for Chester. This latter engine ended its days allocated to 12C Barrow. (R.Picton)

17) Lower semaphore signals abound at Swansea (High Street) station as GWR *Castle* Class 4-6-0 No 5072 *Hurricane* backs onto an up express bound for Paddington after being serviced at its home shed at 87E Landore on 10th April 1950. *Hurricane* remained at Landore until February 1957 when it was drafted to 83D Laira (Plymouth). After April 1958 it spent all but one month allocated to 84A Wolverhampton (Stafford Road), being withdrawn in October 1962. (S.L.C.Philips)

18) The Christmas festivities over and it is back to work as normal at 88D Merthyr on 27th December 1961. As a small group of railwaymen are engaged in conversation resident GWR 5700 Class 0-6-0PT No 9638 is in steam in the shed yard in readiness for its next rostered duty. This small three-road depot was opened in 1877 and closed completely on 2nd November 1964. No 9638 was condemned at the end of 1963 and sent to Cohens, Morriston for scrap. (N.E.Preedy)

19) A wet and miserable summer's day at 6K Rhyl on 26th August 1962 where one of its resident locomotives is noted out of steam in the shed yard. This was the last year of service for the robust and elderly former Lancashire and Yorkshire Railway Class 3F 0-6-0's and No 52119 is only weeks away from withdrawal. Despite the presence of coal in the tender it had been in store since July and was to remain so until scrapped in May 1963. (J.Schatz)

20) The two nearest locomotives in this scene at Abercynon shed on a sunny 11th May 1954 are ex. Taff Vale Railway Class A 0-6-2 Tanks and the third is of the same wheel arrangement. The presence of the two former London and North Western Railway Class 2F 0-6-2 'Coal Tanks' is somewhat intriguing as they are almost certainly shedded at Abergavenny (Brecon Road) at this date in time. No 398, nearest the camera, was withdrawn in August 1957 from 88E. (D.K.Jones)

14

21) Several railwaymen ponder over the problems of rerailing LMS Stanier Class 8F 2-8-0 No 48735, from 87F Llanelly, after a 'mishap' at Knighton station on the Shrewsbury to Ludlow line in March 1961. No 48735 had slipped the rear tender wheels off the track whilst crossing over the points. This locomotive departed from Llanelly shed in September 1964 going to 10D Lostock Hall. Its final abode was at 8E Northwich in Cheshire. (H.H.Bleads)

22) As an unidentified LMS Ivatt Class 2 2-6-0 takes on water supplies in the background whilst in charge of a local passenger train, GWR *Modified Hall* Class 4-6-0 No 6971 *Athelhampton Hall*, allocated to 84E Tyseley in Birmingham, sets off from Shrewsbury with a down express under clear signals which is bound for Chester on an unknown day in 1956. Based at Tyseley for most of its working life, No 6971 was condemned from there in October 1964. (D.K.Jones)

15

23) A close-up look at GWR Churchward 2800 Class 2-8-0 No 2865 which is photographed in bright sunshine in the yard at its home shed at 86A Newport (Ebbw Junction) on 12th June 1949. The 2800 Class of heavy freight engines were first introduced in 1903 and eventually numbered 167 machines some of which had the luxury of side-window cabs. No 2865 survived in revenue earning service until January 1963 being withdrawn from 86E Severn Tunnel Junction. (N.L.Browne)

24) Looking in a rather unkempt condition 8C Speke Junction based LMS Class 5 4-6-0 No 45034 takes an avoiding line at Chester (General) with an up fast fitted freight train on 16th September 1965. Back in the late fifties No 45034 was allocated to 3E Monument Lane in Birmingham until October 1960 when it was moved to 9A Longsight (Manchester) for a brief period of time. After withdrawal from 8C in February 1968 it was cut up at Killamarsh. (B.W.L.Brooksbank)

25) A fine panoramic study of the shed yard and depot structure at the ex. Taff Railway Cardiff (Cathays) on 20th June 1949. A crane occupies the centre road as GWR 5600 Class 0-6-2T No 6660 and an unidentified GWR 1400 Class 0-4-2T simmer in the left of the picture. In the right of the frame is ex. B & M 0-6-2T No 434. Cathays shed (88A) lost its parent status in December 1957 and the bulk of its allocation was transferred to Cardiff (Radyr). (R.S.Carpenter)

26) The 'Dean Goods' could be aptly described at the 'little engines with the big domes' but despite their size over a period of sixty years they compared favourably on test against more modern locomotives. Classified as 2301 0-6-0's they were constructed at Wolverhampton Works and No 2407 of 1891 vintage poses for the camera in the shed yard at Oswestry on 29th July 1951. The last survivor of the class was withdrawn in the late fifties. (B.K.B.Green)

27) A 'stranger in the camp' at 6G Llandudno Junction on 24th July 1964. LNER B1 Class 4-6-0 No 61194, from 41D Canklow, is far from home as it stands alongside the straight running shed. No 61194 had presumably worked through from Sheffield on the Eastern Region with an excursion train. Four months later and this loco was at a new home at 34E New England where it remained until drafted to 40E Colwick. It later became Departmental No 28. (H.L.Holland)

28) Barren hills occupy the high ground as 87A Neath based GWR 5700 Class 0-6-0PT No 3687 passes the diminutive signalbox at the remote and isolated location of Craig-y-Nos (Penwyllt), situated between Colbren Junction and Cray, and enters the station with the 4.10pm local passenger train from Neath to Brecon. This station was to fall an early victim to the 'Beeching Axe' closing during 1962. No 3687 survived at 87A until June 1965. (S.L.C.Philips)

29) The terminus of the North Wales main line is at Holyhead on the island of Anglesey a venue often visited by preserved locomotives even today on steam hauled specials. On a dull day on 2nd May 1964, LMS Class 5 4-6-0 No 44760, from 6G Llandudno Junction, sports empty coaching stock headlamps as it awaits departure light engine. No 44760 made its departure from Llandudno shed in February 1965, moving to London at 1A Willesden. (D.K.Jones)

30) Situated on the south side of the main Chester to North Wales line was the former London and North Western Railway shed at Mold Junction (6B) a couple of minutes walk from the station at Saltney Ferry (closed in 1962). Present in the yard on a sun-filled day on 29th July 1951 is one of its small stud of LMS Stanier Class 6P5F 2-6-0's No 42975. It made its departure from Mold Junction in May 1958 and worked at a host of sheds before withdrawal in March 1966. (B.K.B.Green)

31) We remain on the North Wales main line and our next port of call is Menai Bridge station (closed in 1966) which was once the junction for Anglesey and Afonwen. Standing in front of the entrance to Robert Stephenson's Britannia Tubular Bridge on 20th October 1963 is immaculate looking LMS Fowler Class 4 2-6-4T No 42366 (6AChester) which is being employed on an SLS special. No 42366 was withdrawn in April 1964 and scrapped at Crewe Works. (B.K.B.Green)

32) The Welsh Valleys were at one time riddled with branch lines along with hundreds of remote wayside stations like this one at Cymmer Afon once the property of the little known and long defunct Rhondda and Swansea Bay Railway Company. On a sun-baked 8th June 1963, Cymmer Afon station (closed in 1970) is the subject of a visit by a railway enthusiasts special commanded by GWR 6400 Class 0-6-0PT No 6435 allocated to 88H Tondu. (D.K.Jones)

33) GWR 3400 Class 0-6-0PT No 3400 is seen in steam in the shed yard at 88B Cardiff (Radyr) on 9th May 1964 along with a sister locomotive and resident GWR 5600 Class 0-6-2T No 5635. At this date in time there were seven surviving members of the 3400 Class, Nos 3400-3/5/6/9 and all were allocated to Radyr shed. However, between October and November 1964 all were taken out of traffic and put into store. No 3400 was scrapped at Hayes, Bridgend in early 1965. (D.K.Jones)

34) There is an air of dereliction inside the once busy shed at Abergavenny on 14th August 1957. Once owned by the LNWR it had had its own code under BR - 4D. It lost this during 1955, becoming a sub-shed to 86K Tredegar. On view inside the shed is GWR 6400 Class 0-6-0PT No 6426, from 86G Pontypool Road, and LMS Class 2F 'Webb Coal Tank' 0-6-2T No 58926, of 84G Shrewsbury. Why it has a snowplough at the front in high summer is a mystery! (B.K.B.Green)

35) 26F Patricroft based LMS *Jubilee* Class 4-6-0 No 45600 *Bermuda* looks in superb external fettle as it speeds through Shotton station, situated between Chester and Prestatyn, with the empty stock of special 3Z43 - circa 1962. *Bermuda*, a longstanding resident at Patricroft shed in Manchester, finally departed from there in January 1965 when it moved the few miles to 9D Newton Heath. By the end of the year it was condemned and placed in store at 9D. (Kit Windle)

36) Deep in the heart of the Welsh Valleys GWR 2800 Class 2-8-0 No 3850 is halted by a signal at Aberdare as it powers a mineral train tender-first on 21st September 1962. Based locally, No 3850 had been at Aberdare shed since a move from 86E Severn Tunnel Junction in February 1959. It remained there until November 1963 when it was drafted to the Midlands at 2D Banbury. Before withdrawal in August 1965 it also worked from 6E Oswestry and 6C Croes Newydd. (D.K.Jones)

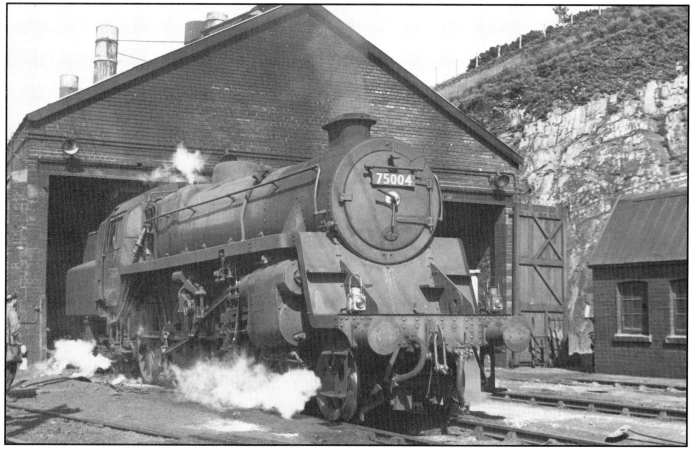

37) High bluffs look down upon the railway scene at 6F Machynlleth where we espy BR Class 4 4-6-0 No 75004 (equipped with a double chimney) being prepared to work an express duty in July 1965. Machynlleth shed (Cambrian Railways), opened in 1863, was owned by the Western Region from 1948 to September 1963 and coded 89C. It then became the property of the London Midland Region up until closure in December 1966. Its surviving stock was transferred away. (R.W.Hinton)

38) Transferred from 81A Old Oak Common to 86C Cardiff (Canton) in August 1960, GWR *King* Class 4-6-0 No 6003 *King George IV* powers the lengthy 1.55pm express from Paddington to Milford Haven at Severn Tunnel Junction on 17th June 1961. Between August 1960 and October 1961 a total of eight *Kings* were drafted to Canton shed, these being Nos. 6003/4/10/18/19/23/24/28. *King George IV* was withdrawn from Canton in June 1962 after completing 1,920,479 miles. (R.Picton)

39) The line from Barmouth to Ruabon via Dolgelly has long since closed, but the section from Barmouth to Aberystwyth and Shrewsbury via Dovey Junction is still with us today albeit with diesel traction. On 7th August 1959 GWR 4300 Class 2-6-0 No 5351 skirts the estuary at Barmouth as it heads a four-coach stopping train bound for Ruabon. Allocated to 84C Banbury, No 5351 was drafted to 81E Didcot a month after this picture was taken. (N.E.Preedy)

40) Begrimed and work-stained LMS Hughes Class 6P5F 'Crab' 2-6-0 No 42759 is an unusual visitor to 89B Croes Newdd (Wrexham) from 9G Gorton in Manchester on 22nd September 1962. Once of 14A Cricklewood, No 42759 had been moved to 17B Burton in January 1959. It remained at Burton until transferred to Gorton in March 1961. By January 1963 it was one of a numerical batch allocated to 9G, Nos 42757-61. It was withdrawn from Gorton during this same month. (N.E.Preedy)

41) Rhymney Railway A Class 0-6-2T No 19 as GWR No 59 at 88C Barry on 19th June 1949. Designed by Mr. Hurry-Riches to replace older Saddle Tank Classes at Rhymney, Dowlais and Merthyr they were re-boilered by the GWR following Grouping. They were very successful with the standard No 10 boiler and many of the class survived into the fifties. No 59, which lasted until 1955, is seen in early British Railways livery with plain lettering. (A.N.H.Glover)

42) The regulator is opened and BR Class 3 2-6-2T No 82032, from 89A Shrewsbury, blasts out of Aberystwyth with a local passenger train bound for Machynlleth on 22nd September 1962. No 82032 had a number of homes during its relatively short career. Apart from Shrewsbury it was based at 88F Treherbert, 88A Cardiff (Radyr), 82A Bristol (Bath Road), 6E Chester, (GWR), 6A Chester (LMR), 89C Machynlleth and 6H Bangor. It was withdrawn from the latter in May 1965. (N.E.Preedy)

43) 85B Gloucester (Horton Road) based GWR Castle Class 4-6-0 No 5094 *Tretower Castle* is a visitor to 84G Shrewsbury during 1957 where it is seen in steam in the shed yard. *Tretower Castle* was despatched to the Bristol area in August 1960 where it served from the sheds at Bath Road and St.Philip's Marsh. Fitted with a double chimney in June 1960 it fell victim to the great slaughter of steam in September 1962. It was scrapped at Cashmores, Newport. (D.K.Jones)

44) Although it is almost winter there is bright sunshine at Pembroke Dock station in November 1961. Newly transferred to 87H Neyland from 87G Carmarthen, GWR *Manor* Class 4-6-0 No 7825 *Lechlade Manor* stands in the shadows with the stock of a passenger train. Today, no less than nine of these handsome engines are preserved. Unfortunately *Lechlade Manor* is not one of them for after being withdrawn in May 1964 from 81D Reading it was scrapped at Birds, Risca. (D.K.Jones)

45) Shortly before being drafted to 5A Crewe (North), LMS *Royal Scot* Class 4-6-0 No 46155 *The Lancer*, from 6G Llandudno Junction, drifts along beneath a characterless concrete footbridge on the approach to Deganwy station in the latter section of its journey from Chester to Llandudno with a lengthy express on 8th June 1963. In October 1964 *The Lancer* was drafted to a new home at 12A Carlisle (Kingmoor), but its stay was shortlived and it was soon withdrawn. (T.R.Amos)

46) Colour light signals guard the eastern exit at Cardiff (General) station on 16th September 1962. Awaiting departure with a Swansea (High Street) to Paddington express is GWR *Castle* Class 4-6-0 No 5001 *Llandovery Castle*, from 81A Old Oak Common, seen here with a straight-sided tender. Although looking in good condition it was condemned from 81A in February 1963 and after a period of storage at Old Oak and 81F Oxford it was cut up at Cashmores, Great Bridge. (J.Schatz)

47) The 'Dukedog' GWR 9000 Class 2P 4-4-0's as they were nicknamed, worked mostly over the former Cambrian Railways system on passenger trains and in 1948 at the inception of British Railways there were twenty-seven of them still in service. In January 1957 there were still twenty-two of them at work based at Croes Newydd, Machynlleth, Oswestry and Swindon. One example, No 9001, is seen in bright sunshine at Oswestry depot on 30th August 1953. (B.K.B.Green)

48) Its bunker filled to the brim with coal supplies, GWR 5600 Class 0-6-2T No 6632 awaits its next duty in a siding at its home base at 89B Croes Newydd on 2nd September 1962. This shed, of Great Western origin, consisted of a single covered roundhouse situated in a triangle of lines. Coded 84J and 89B whilst under Western Region control it was recoded to 6C when the London Midland Region took charge in September 1963. Closure came in June 1967. (J.Schatz)

49) With the empty coaching stock of a Paddington-Newport-Cardiff-Swansea-Neyland express near at hand one of the small stud of GWR *County* Class 4-6-0's based at the nearby shed of 87H, No 1020 *County of Monmouth*, stands in the platform at Neyland station with a local passenger working on 4th August 1960. In October 1962 this locomotive (equipped with a double chimney in November 1958) was reallocated to a new home at 82B St.Philip's Marsh. (D.K.Jones)

50) For many years an inhabitant at 18C Hasland LMS Kitson Class 0F 0-4-0ST No 47003 was drafted to Wales where it was based as a docks shunter at 87D Swansea East Dock from July 1963 up until withdrawal in April 1964. No 47003 is seen at 87D on 19th August 1963 and its driver looks towards the camera. Whether he was bemused by the allocation of this 'foreigner', complete with a warning bell over the cab, we shall never know. (H.L.Holland)

51) GWR Dean 1854 Class 0-6-0PT No 1891, built at Swindon Works in the same year (as No 1218), is noted in store parked in a siding at 86C Cardiff (Canton) on 19th June 1949 shortly after withdrawal. Canton shed in steam days was a huge affair with a massive allocation from the humblest of engines like No 1891 to the mighty GWR *Kings* and BR *Britannias*. In September 1962 it was closed to steam and today it is still in use as a diesel depot. (A.N.H.Glover)

52) Bright sunlight and deep shadow at Saltney Junction a few short miles from Chester on 20th July 1963. Approaching the camera is LMS Class 5 4-6-0 No 45311, from 6G Llandudno Junction and in ex.works condition, which is in charge of a heavily laden summer extra. Once of 5B Crewe (South), 5D Stoke and 5A Crewe (North), No 45311 had been at Llandudno Junction shed since May 1962. Its last home was at 6D Shrewsbury from whence it was withdrawn in October 1966. (D.K.Jones)

53) Trains from Paddington to Chester and Birkenhead always called at Gobowen, for it was the junction for Oswestry and the Cambrian line to the Welsh coastal resorts. With Gobowen station in the distance GWR *Hall* Class 4-6-0 No 5914 *Ripon Hall*, from 85B Gloucester (Horton Road), heads towards Chirk and Chester with a semi-fast service on 31st August 1963. Within less than five months *Ripon Hall* was no longer with us, withdrawn and unwanted. (Peter Hay)

54) Although the shadows are lengthening there is still bright sunshine which is reflecting off former Taff Vale Railway A Class 0-6-2T No 307. Built at the Vulcan Foundry in 1929 as No 415, it was rebuilt by the Great Western Railway in 1929 at Caerphilly Works and was withdrawn by British Railways in March 1956. One of fifty plus locomotives designed mainly for passenger work, No 307 is seen in the yard at 88A Cardiff (Cathays) on 7th June 1953. (F.Hornby)

55) For many years, outside of West Wales, the locomotive featured here was an elusive beast for trainspotters and photographers alike being allocated to the remote outpost at 87J Goodwick in Fishguard. GWR *Hall* Class 4-6-0 No 4981 *Abberley Hall* is noted out of steam in the shed yard at 87J on 4th June 1960. When Goodwick shed closed in September 1963, *Abberley Hall* was drafted to 81F Oxford but it was withdrawn the following month. (N.E.Preedy)

56) A wisp of steam escapes from the safety valves of Riddles War Department Class 8F 2-8-0 No 90398, from 24B Rose Grove, as it trundles through Chester station and passes No 3A signalbox with a mixed freight on 20th July 1963. Once of 24C Lostock Hall, 90398 had made its way to Rose Grove shed via 26D Bury in August 1962. Before condemnation in July 1965 it also served from the sheds at 9D Newton Heath, 10H Lower Darwen and 41J Langwith Junction. (D.K.Jones)

57) Former Taff Vale Railway A Class 0-6-2T No 383 looks in fine external condition as it stands in bright sunshine in the yard of its home shed at 88E Abercynon on 13th June 1957. Despite its fine condition it was withdrawn two months later. Abercynon shed was opened in 1929 by the GWR, replacing an earlier Taff Vale structure. It was closed completely on 2nd November 1964 and its remaining stock was transferred to other depots in South Wales. (D.K.Jones)

58) Although thoroughly 'Westernised', GWR 0-6-2T No 284 began life in 1910 as Taff Vale Railway No 35 of Class OX. Designed by Mr. Hurry-Riches in 1907, the class totalled forty-one units of which a handful survived into 1955. No 284, in ex.works condition, is seen at 86J Aberdare in April 1952. Aberdare shed was a single turntable depot located on the northern side of the Low Level station. It closed completely on 1st March 1965. (D.K.Jones)

59) Less than two years old, GWR *Castle* Class 4-6-0 No 7008 *Swansea Castle*, allocated to 81A Old Oak Common, steams into Newport (High Street) station with a down express from Paddington on 10th April 1950. Apart from a brief foray at 81F Oxford in the early sixties, *Swansea Castle* remained based at 81A for all of its short life in which it only covered 483,663 miles. Equipped with a double chimney in May 1959 it was withdrawn in September 1964. (S.L.C.Philips)

60) Precisely what GWR 5700 Class 0-6-0PT No 9637 (87E Landore) is doing in front of GWR *Castle* Class 4-6-0 No 5077 *Fairy Battle* (also from Landore) at Swansea (High Street) station on 1st May 1961 is not known. Two months later Landore closed to steam prior to becoming a diesel depot and both Nos 5077 and 9637 were on the move. They were moved to a new abode at 87F Llanelly from where *Fairy Battle* was withdrawn in July 1962 after 24 years of service. (D.K.Jones)

61) Almost the last of their line two 'bulled-up' GWR 5700 Class 0-6-0 Pannier Tanks, Nos 9630 and 9610 are seen in steam in the yard at 6C Croes Newydd on 21st August 1966. Note the home-made front numberplate on No 9630. The pair had been employed on a Stephenson Locomotive Society special from Birmingham (Snow Hill). Withdrawn from 6C the following month both were stored at 2A Tyseley prior to scrapping at Cashmores, Great Bridge. (N.E.Preedy)

62) With a member of the footplate crew looking towards the camera GWR *Manor* Class 4-6-0 No 7827 *Lydham Manor*, from 89D Oswestry, leaks steam as it approaches Aberystwyth with a partially fitted freight in June 1962. In the extreme right of the picture is a tabletcatcher. No 7827 ended its days at 6D Shrewsbury being withdrawn in October 1965. After withdrawal it was stored at Barry Docks before being saved by the Torbay Steam Railway. (N.L.Browne)

63) On a bright early summer's day LMS Class 5 4-6-0 No 45132, allocated to 6B Mold Junction, trundles along the North Wales main line at Colwyn Bay with a down goods train on 7th June 1952. Later on in life No 45132 was based at 3D Aston, 5A Crewe (North), 5D Stoke and 6J Holyhead. As with *Lydham Manor* in the previous picture it ended its days at 6D Shrewsbury, being condemned in March 1967. It was scrapped at Cohens, Morriston in October 1967. (N.E.Preedy)

64) Fresh from overhaul at one of the Western Region workshops, GWR Hawksworth 9400 Class 0-6-0PT No 9426 is on parade in the yard of its home shed at 86C Cardiff (Canton) on 20th September 1955. No 9426 remained at Canton until the closure of the shed to steam, moving to the re-opened depot at 88L Cardiff East Dock. Twelve months or so later it was at 88C Barry followed by a final move to 88B Cardiff (Radyr) in October 1964. (B.K.B.Green)

65) A brace of begrimed GWR *Grange* Class 4-6-0's occupy one of the roads at 87F Llanelly on 16th September 1962. Nearest the camera is No 6804 *Brockington Grange*, a local steed, behind which is No 6832 *Brockton Grange*, from 87A Neath. The *Granges* were virtually unaffected by the mass withdrawals of 1962 and by the end of 1963 only nine had been condemned. No 6832 was withdrawn in January 1964 followed by No 6804 seven months later. (J.Schatz)

66) Once part of the proud fleet once allocated to 86C Cardiff (Canton), BR *Britannia* Class 4-6-2 No 70015 *Apollo* had arrived at 5A Crewe (North) via 9E Trafford Park, 26A Newton Heath, 14D Neasden, 16D Annesley, 1A Willesden and 6G Llandudno Junction in September 1963. It is seen here at Chester station passing a rake of empty stock with an excursion in August 1964 from Euston to Holyhead. It was withdrawn from service in August 1967. (Kit Windle)

67) A crowd of young spotters mill around one of the platforms at Shrewsbury (no wonder we were ejected from stations!) on 16th June 1962. The main subject of the photographer's attention is 88A Cardiff (Canton) based GWR *Castle* Class 4-6-0 No 5021 *Whittington Castle*, seen here paired with a straight-sided tender. *Whittington Castle* was yet another GWR type to fall victim to the heavy withdrawals in September 1962. (D.K.Jones)

68) The fireman has the single line tablet at the ready as the pioneer GWR *Manor* Class 4-6-0 No 7800 *Torquay Manor*, from 6E Chester (West), glides into Barmouth station with the 12.11pm local passenger train from Ruabon on 17th July 1958. During the following month *Torquay Manor* was transferred to a new home at 89A Oswestry where it remained until February 1963, moving to 89A Shrewsbury, its final abode, being withdrawn in August 1964. (F.Hornby)

69) A trio of local GWR 5700 Class 0-6-0 Pannier Tanks are noted in the shed yard at 88C Barry on 13th August 1957. From left to right are Nos 6746 (withdrawn in August 1958), 4610 withdrawn from 83D Exmouth Junction in October 1964 after spells at 73H Dover, 70B Feltham and 71G Weymouth and 6733 (withdrawn in May 1958). Opened by the Barry Railway in 1888, Barry shed closed in September 1964 and its survivors were transferred to 88B Cardiff (Radyr). (B.K.B.Green)

70) Steam a' plenty in the shed yard at 86E Severn Tunnel Junction on 8th August 1961. The main focus of the photographer's attention is 81A Old Oak Common based GWR *Modified Hall* Class 4-6-0 No 6978 *Haroldstone Hall*. A longstanding resident of 81A, *Haroldstone Hall* had a flurry of transfers from October 1963 to February 1965 moving to 81C Southall, back to Old Oak Common, on to 86E Severn Tunnel Junction and finally to 86B Newport (Ebbw Junction). (N.E.Preedy)

71) With a weed-strewn platform in the left of the frame some of the occupants of this Locomotive Club of Great Britain special at Blaenau Festiniog in the heart of Snowdonia go for a walk-about in the sun on 24th September 1966. In charge of the train is a double-header consisting of two LMS Class 4 2-6-4 Tanks, Nos 42574 and 42644, both from 9E Trafford Park. Of the two, No 42574 survived the longest being withdrawn in October 1967. (B.K.B. Green)

72) It is the 25th September 1965 and the end is almost nigh for the long association with the steam locomotive in South Wales. A crowd of onlookers has gathered to pay their last respects at Colbren Junction on the former Neath and Brecon Railway, the station of which had closed in 1962. Employed on a railway enthusiasts special are a brace of GWR 5700 Class 0-6-0 Pannier Tanks, Nos 3654, from 88A Cardiff East Dock, and 9609, from 87F Llanelly. (J.Schatz)

73) As the sixties progressed sights like this one became commonplace as steam locomotives were placed into store at their respective depots in droves, awaiting the final call to the scrapyard. In June 1965 five LMS Class 2 2-6-2 Tanks stand together steamless and unwanted with sacked chimneys on the store line at 6G Llandudno Junction. Officially condemned two months after this picture was taken, No 41232 leads the line-up. (N.L.Browne)

74) Designed by Fowler the LMS Class 3 2-6-2 Tanks, first introduced in 1930, eventually numbered a total of seventy engines, some of which were fitted with condensing apparatus and used through the tunnels radiating from Moorgate station in London. They were scattered far and wide at depots on three regions of BR, including 84G Shrewsbury, which is home to No 40058 on 30th August 1953. It was withdrawn in November 1959 from 6G Llandudno Junction. (B.K.B.Green)

75) Looking in fine fettle GWR *Castle* Class 4-6-0 No 5038 *Morlais Castle*, from 84G Shrewsbury, climbs up from the depths of the Severn tunnel and approaches Pilning with a Liverpool to Plymouth express on 12th May 1958. Transferred to Shrewsbury the previous month, *Morlais Castle* stayed there until May 1962 moving to 81F Oxford. In October of the same year it went to a final home at 81D Reading from where it was condemned in September 1963. (N.E.Preedy)

76) Parked in a siding at Towyn, near to Tremadoc Bay, is GWR 'Dukedog' Class 2P 4-4-0 No 9017, based at 89C Machynlleth, in August 1957. This was the last example of the class to be withdrawn, from 89C in October 1960. Stored at 89D Oswestry for a long time it has been preserved for many years on the Bluebell Railway. Accompanying No 9017 is Oswestry based BR Class 4 4-6-0 No 75024 which survived in service until November 1967. (D.K.Jones)

77) Paired with a straight-sided tender, GWR *Hall* Class 4-6-0 No 6934 *Beachamwell Hall*, from 89A Shrewsbury, steams through Wrexham (General) station under clear signals with the 8.05am express from Paddington to Birkenhead (Woodside) on 3rd August 1963. Once of 84B Oxley, *Beachamwell Hall* had also served at 84A Wolverhampton (Stafford Road) before moving to Shrewsbury in April 1961. It ended its days at 2D Banbury being withdrawn in October 1965. (J.M.Tolson)

78) LMS Class 6P5F 'Crab' 2-6-0 No 42942, of 8H Birkenhead, stands in Denbigh station (closed in 1962) whilst being employed on an LCGB special on 24th September 1966. Note the gantry behind No 42942 stripped of signals. No 42942 was one of a handful of survivors from the class at this stage in time and along with No 42727 it was the last to be withdrawn, from 8H in January 1967. It was cut up at Cashmores, Great Bridge later in the year. (B.K.B.Green)

79) A panoramic view of the yard and running shed at 6B Mold Junction on 8th June 1963. Amongst the locomotives on view are LMS Class 6P5F 2-6-0 No 42984, from 5B Crewe (South), LMS CLass 6P5F 'Crab' 2-6-0 No 42783 (6C Birkenhead), LMS Class 8F 2-8-0 No 48441, also from Birkenhead, along with sister engines Nos 48455 and 48749, both local engines, and GWR *Hall* Class 4-6-0 No 4943 *Marrington Hall*, which was withdrawn from 86G Pontypool Road late in 1963. (T.R.Amos)

80) Sunlight and shadow at Pontypool Road on 21st May 1955 where locally based (86G) GWR 5600 Class 0-6-2T No 6636 heads
     a rake of empty coaching stock. Having noted that the former South Wales railway companies prefered the 0-6-2T wheel
     arrangement for both freight and local passenger workings, Collett put into service 200 engines of this class between 1924 and
     1928. No 6636 survived at Pontypool Road shed until June 1963. (F.Hornby)

81) The last but one member of the GWR *Castle* Class 4-6-0's No 7036 *Taunton Castle*, from 81A Old Oak Common, awaits departure from Cardiff (General) station on 20th August 1961 with the 2.00pm express for Paddington. Emerging from Swindon Works on 18th August 1950, *Taunton Castle*, equipped with a double chimney in July 1959, only amassed 617,653 miles during its short working life. It was condemned from Old Oak Common in September 1963. (R.Picton)

82) A fine panoramic view of the shed at 87C Danygraig, opened in 1896, where we espy GWR 9400 Class 0-6-0PT No 9487, GWR 5700 Class 0-6-0PT No 8720, Swansea Harbour Trust 0-4-0ST No 1142, GWR 1101 Class 0-4-0T No 1104, Llanelly and Mynydd Mawr 0-6-0T No 359 *Hilda* and Swansea Harbour Trust 0-4-0ST No 1143 parked in front of the depot on 7th June 1953. The shed consisted of four running roads with a locomotive carriage and wagon shops. (N.L.Browne)

83) Black smoke is blasted into the sky as GWR 4300 Class 2-6-0 No 6345, from far off 88A Cardiff (Canton), attacks the stiff gradient on Gresford bank, near Wrexham, with a lengthy Birkenhead to Barmouth local passenger train in the summer of 1961. When Canton shed closed to steam, No 6345 moved to 88L Cardiff East Dock in September 1962. In December 1963 it moved to 83B Taunton and worked on the Barnstaple route until withdrawn in September 1964. (Denis Lewis)

84) Equipped with a double chimney nine months earlier and paired with a straight-sided tender, GWR *Castle* Class 4-6-0 No 5078 *Beaufort*, of 87A Neath, stands in Swansea (High Street) station with the 6.45am express from Fishguard to Paddington on 16th September 1962. Built at Swindon Works in May 1939, *Beaufort* was originally named *Lamphey Castle*. It was withdrawn from Neath shed two months after this picture was taken and was cut up in 1963 at Swindon. (J.Schatz)

85) BR Class 2 2-6-0 No 78059 stands in the yard of its home shed at 6H Bangor on 20th May 1962 in the company of an unidentified LMS Class 4F 0-6-0. This shed, of London and North Western Railway origin, was a six-road affair situated alongside the station at Bangor. Originally coded 7B by BR it closed on 14th June 1965. No 78059 ended its days based at 5A Crewe (North) and after many years of storage at Barry Docks it has been saved for posterity. (D.Harrison)

86) GWR Churchward heavy freight 2800 Class 2-8-0 No 2894, fitted with a side-window cab, stands in a section of the yard at its home shed of 86A Newport (Ebbw Junction) on 7th April 1963. Opened by the GWR in July 1915 it was a massive affair with a twin covered roundhouse and a large repair shop. Situated on the north side of the main line about a mile from Newport station it was a forty-five minute walk for those spotters who were keen enough for a visit. (N.E.Preedy)

87) The GWR 4400 Class 2-6-2 Tanks first arrived on the railway scene in 1904 and the eleven locomotives constructed were primarily designed for work on steeply graded lines. No 4406 is seen in the yard at 86F Tondu which was its home base on an unknown day in 1952. This depot, a single covered roundhouse opened in 1889, was situated in a triangle of lines between Tondu station, Tondu North Junction and Ogmore Junction. It closed in April 1964. (L.Brownhill)

88) Under grey skies after a heavy shower GWR 4500 Class 2-6-2T No 4501, from 89C Machynlleth, stands in Machynlleth station with an up local on 3rd August 1951. The view we have here is looking west towards Dovey Junction. These were very popular and versatile engines from a design of 1906. Some were built with inside steampipes, but eventually all had outside steampipes. No 4501 was withdrawn from service before the fifties came to a close. (B.W.L.Brooksbank)

89) A member of the footplate crew of LMS *Royal Scot* Class 4-6-0 No 46120 *Royal Inniskilling Fusilier*, allocated to 6G Llandudno Junction, looks out of the cab of his charge as it enters Chester (General) station with an express on a soaking wet 3rd August 1962. Records show us that No 46120 was also based at 5A Crewe (North), 1B Camden, 9A Longsight (Manchester) and 1A Willesden between January 1957 and its withdrawal from service in July 1963. (D.K.Jones)

90) Located on the west side of the Taff Vale main line between Llandaff and Radyr stations was the depot at Cardiff (Radyr), coded 88A and 88B under British Railways. It had a large allocation all of which consisted of tank engine types like GWR 5700 Class 0-6-0PT No 8780 seen here in bright sunshine in the yard on 8th August 1951. Withdrawn in July 1962 it was stored at both Radyr and Caerphilly Works before being scrapped in June 1963. (N.E.Preedy)

91) Although less than twenty years old it is the end of the road for GWR *County* Class 4-6-0 No 1001 *County of Bucks*, fitted with a double chimney in December 1957, as it awaits its final journey to the breakers yard at 87H Neyland on 17th September 1963, some four months after withdrawal. For many years a Neyland steed, *County of Bucks* was based at 83G Penzance from January 1961 until September 1962, returning to Neyland for a final stint. (D.K.Jones)

92) GWR *Hall* Class 4-6-0 No 4913 *Baglan Hall*, a local engine from 86C, is seen on a centre track at Hereford on l9th September 1961 where it is attaching/detaching vehicles from a parcels train. Named after the Hall which once stood near Port Talbot, No 4913 had been allocated to the sheds at 84B Oxley, 84G Shrewsbury, 83D Laira (Plymouth), 81D Reading and 81E Didcot prior to moving to Hereford in December 1959. It died there in September 1962. (N.E.Preedy)

93) Another Hereford based GWR *Hall* Class 4-6-0 No 5998 *Trevor Hall* glides past a group of railway workers with a rake of 'blood and custard' coaches as it arrives at Shrewsbury with an express in the mid-fifties. For a brief period of time from June to July 1958 *Trevor Hall* was allocated to 84G Shrewsbury before returning to Hereford shed until November 1963. A final transfer then took it to 86G Pontypool Road where it was condemned in March 1964. (D.K.Jones)

94) GWR inspired but British Railways built 1600 Class 0-6-0PT No 1638 stands in bright sunshine alongside its home shed at 89D Oswestry in company with an unidentified LMS Class 2 2-6-0 on 9th June 1963. No 1638 had been moved to Oswestry in August 1962 after many years at 87F Llanelly. In January 1965 it was on the move again, this time to 6C Croes Newydd where it was condemned in August 1966. Since 1967 it has been preserved on the Dart Valley Railway. (N.E.Preedy)

95) GWR 9400 Class 0-6-0PT No 9425 stands outside the six-road shed at 88C Barry in the company of a sister engine on a sun-filled 19th March 1960. Once of 88F Treherbert and 88A Cardiff (Radyr), No 9425 had been allocated to 88C since March 1959. It was destined to remain here until August 1963 moving to 86F Aberbeeg where its stay was rather shortlived to say the least, being condemned three months later and cut up at Swindon Works. (N.E.Preedy)

96) With a large slagheap in the background 87E Landore (Swansea) based GWR *Castle* Class 4-6-0 No 7009 *Athelney Castle* stands in the yard of its home shed with a GWR 0-6-0 Pannier Tank in September 1954. Coupled to a straight-sided tender this May 1948 constructed engine parted company with Landore shed in September 1960, moving to 87G Carmarthen. It later served from 85A Worcester, 85B Gloucester (Horton Road) and 81A Old Oak Common (twice). (L.Brownhill)

97) Another 87E Landore based locomotive, GWR *Castle* Class 4-6-0 No 5041 *Tiverton Castle* pauses at Cardiff (General) with the up *Red Dragon* express bound for Paddington on an unknown day in 1956. Upon the closure of 87E to steam in June 1961, *Tiverton Castle* was drafted to 87G Carmarthen. Twelve months or so later it was at its final base at 81A Old Oak Common, being withdrawn from there in December 1963 after completing 1,383,804 miles. (R.W.Hinton)

98) Travelling bunker-first GWR 5101 Class 2-6-2T No 4108, from 88H Tondu, arrives at Bridgend station with its two-coach load forming the 2.33pm local passenger from Blaengwynfi on the former Rhondda and Swansea Railway on 19th November 1962. Prior to being allocated to Tondu in September 1960, No 4108 had been based at 84A Wolverhampton (Stafford Road) in the Midlands and at 83A Newton Abbot and 83F Truro in the West Country. (J.Schatz)

99) As an unidentified BR Class 4 4-6-0 awaits clearance for departure BR Class 4 2-6-4T No 80105, from 6F Machynlleth, arrives at Barmouth Junction on a misty 17th July 1964 with a local passenger service. Once of the Eastern Region at 33A Plaistow and 33B Tilbury, No 80105 had been drafted to the Western Region in September 1962. After withdrawal in July 1965 it was stored at Barry until October 1973, being saved by the Scottish R.P.S. (R.Picton)

100) Locally based GWR 5600 Class 0-6-2T No 5675 is coaled and ready for its next duty inside the gloom of one of the two roundhouses at 87F Llanelly on 8th May 1964 some seven months before being condemned. During the late fifties No 5675 served from the motive power depots at 81E Didcot and 81D Reading before moving to South Wales at 88A Cardiff (Radyr) in January 1959. It also worked from 87D Swansea East Dock for a number of years. (D.K.Jones)

101) Paired with a Great Central Railway style of tender, GWR 2251 Class 0-6-0 No 2202, of 89C Machynlleth, is in charge of a local passenger service at Welshpool, situated approximately half-way between Shrewsbury and Moat Lane Junction on the former Cambrian Railways, on a sunny 24th August 1957. No 2202 had a brief fling at 89A Oswestry from December 1958 until January 1959 before returning to 89C, being withdrawn from there in October 1960. (D.K.Jones)

102) Based locally at 86A Ebbw Junction, GWR 5101 Class 2-6-2T No 4168 looks in splendid external condition as it stands at Newport (High Street) with a local passenger working on 12th July 1951. No 4168 made its departure from Ebbw Junction shed in December 1957 moving to new surroundings at 84F Stourbridge where it remained for many years until July 1965. Its final base was at 2A Tyseley from whence it was condemned in September 1965. (N.E.Preedy)

103) In the latter days of steam the working survivors were rarely cleaned, partly because of the shortage of cleaners and partly because of the apathy of the 'modern image' authorities to whom 'steam' was a dirty word. Looking suitably neglected at Wrexham in September 1966 is an unidentified former Crosti-boilered BR Class 9F 2-10-0 and a sister engine in more conventional form, No 92135 from 6C Croes Newydd. (R.Butterfield)

104) When the ex. London and North Western Railway shed at Swansea (Victoria) closed in situ on 31st August 1959 the bulk of its stud of LMS Class 8F 2-8-0's were transferred to 87F Llanelly where a handful of them continued to work into 1965. On 14th October 1962 one of their ranks, No 48706, its shedcode crudely stencilled on the smokebox door, it noted in the yard at 86G Pontypool Road. It took its leave of Llanelly in May 1965. (N.E.Preedy)

105) A crowded scene within the confines of the yard at 6B Mold Junction on 10th October 1960. In the left of the frame is locally based LMS Class 3F 0-6-0T No 47410 an inmate of 6B since March of this same year following a move from 24L Carnforth. In February 1964 it found a new and final home at 6J Holyhead, being condemned from there in September 1966. The main focus of attention is on GWR 2800 Class 2-8-0 No 3806, from 86A Newport (Ebbw Junction). (N.E.Preedy)

106) GWR 2800 Class 2-8-0 No 3864, of 86E Severn Tunnel Junction, leaks steam as it labours up the gradient and passes Cattybrook brickworks with the aid of rear end assistance with a lengthy goods train on 5th September 1963. No 3864 had been based in the West Country at 83A Newton Abbot for a number of years before moving to 86E in May 1960. Prior to withdrawal in July 1965 it also worked from 87A Neath and 86B Newport (Ebbw Junction). (R.Picton)

107) Bleak hills look down upon the rows and rows of terraced houses at Swansea East Dock and into the shed yard on an unknown day in June 1961. Shortly after being transferred to 87D from 87E Landore are a duet of LMS Fowler Class 4 2-6-4 Tanks, Nos 42305 and 42388 which are lined up in the yard. Withdrawn in September and October 1962 respectively, these former Swansea (Victoria) locomotives were both cut up at Derby Works. (D.K.Jones)

108) A trio of former Rhymney Railway 0-6-2 Tanks, Nos 77, 78 and 83 are parked on or near to the turntable at the Bargoed end of the cramped three-road shed at Rhymney on 1st August 1953. All three locomotives had been modified with taper boilers by the Great Western Railway. Rhymney was a sub-shed of 88D Merthyr for many years and was situated alongside its own station. It took over the code of 88D in November 1964 a few months before closure. (W.Potter)

109) The peace and tranquillity of the heavily wooded countryside on the English-Welsh border near to Wrexham is disturbed momentarily as GWR *Castle* Class 4-6-0 No 5088 *Llanthony Castle*, from 84A Wolverhampton (Stafford Road), clambers up Gresford bank with the 4.45pm semi-fast passenger train from Birkenhead to Paddington on 16th June 1957. Modified with a double chimney in June 1958, No 5088 was to fall victim to the mass withdrawals of September 1962. (Denis Lewis)

110) A clear view of the frontage and inside of the shed at 88D Merthyr with its corrugated facia on 8th September 1961. Standing in front of the shed is resident GWR 5600 Class 0-6-2T No 5677 which remained at Merthyr shed until September 1962, moving to 87A Neath. In November 1964 it was reallocated to Rhymney shed, with its new code of 88D, remaining there until forced to a new abode at 6C Croes Newydd after the closure of 88D in May 1965. (T.R.Amos)

111) Constructed at Swindon Works in July 1932, GWR *Castle* Class 4-6-0 No 5017 was originally named *St.Donats Castle*, but in April 1954 it was renamed *The Gloucestershire Regiment 28th 61st* as a tribute to the heroic exploits of the 'Glorious Gloucesters' during the Korean War. It was also allocated to 85B Gloucester (Horton Road) for many years up until withdrawal in September 1962 and is seen at Cardiff (General) on 24th June 1958. (D.K.Jones)

112) Nowadays more well known as the home for the 'Royal Mint', Llantrisant, some 156 miles from Paddington, used to be the junction of lines leading to Aberthaw (closed to passenger in 1964) and Penygraig, which lost its passenger services in 1958. On 12th May 1964, GWR 4200 Class 2-8-0T No 5261, from 88A Cardiff East Dock, steams quietly through Llantrisant with a heavy freight duty. No 5261 was withdrawn from 88A in March 1965. (D.K.Jones)

113) The GWR 4300 Class 2-6-0's, with their light axle weight, were able to work over most of the Western Region system and were to be seen mostly on freight and local passenger workings. The lines they were mostly at home on were the single track secondary ones such as the once numerous ones in Devon, West Wales and the Cambrian system. After many years of working over the latter, No 6339 lies condemned at 89B Croes Newydd in September 1962. (N.E.Preedy)

114) Such was the density of traffic in South Wales during steam days that there were a host of sub-sheds, some quite large and others not so big. Falling into the latter category is the one-road structure at Glyn Neath (sub to 87A Neath). It was opened by the GWR in 1879 and closed for ever on 5th October 1964. Its main use was a base for banking engines and in this picture we espy two GWR 4200 Class 2-8-0 Tanks, Nos 4281 and 5239 on 19th April 1953. (B.K.B.Green)

115) Both sporting special excursion reporting numbers, a brace of GWR 5600 Class 0-6-2 Tanks have been called upon to provide power for trains to Barry Island and 'all the fun of the fair' on 19th June 1960. Both are on shed at 88C Barry and the nearest can be identified as No 6629, from 86H Aberbeeg. As the sixties progressed and the motor car came into fashion, excursions like this soon declined as did No 6629 in October 1962. (A.N.H.Glover)

116) Despite its smart condition 86E Severn Tunnel Junction based GWR *Grange* Class 4-6-0 No 6859 *Yiewsley Grange* is less than two months away from withdrawal as it prepares to leave with the 10.00am joint RCTS/SLS special to Fishguard and back with what was to have been the final steam departure from Swansea (High Street) on 20th September 1965. Twenty years to the day (almost) and, thanks to the preservation movement, steam was seen again at Swansea. (D.I.John)

117) Staying on the subject of the 'preservation movement' we can thank the same organisation for saving GWR *Manor* Class 4-6-0 No 7820 *Dinmore Manor* from the cutter's torch after many years of rotting away at Barry Docks. In the summer of 1963, *Dinmore Manor*, from 89C Machynlleth and minus shedplate, arrives at Barmouth under clear signals with a short freight. After a spell at 84B Oxley it was withdrawn from 6D Shrewsbury in November 1965. (Kit Windle)

118) The GWR 5700 Class 0-6-0 Pannier Tanks were the shunting workhorse of the Great Western and Western Regions of BR. There was hardly a freight yard, passenger station or line on the system where they were not present. In January 1957 some 860 of these engines were still in service, numerically the largest single class of locomotives on BR. On 12th July 1959, No 3762, from 87B Duffryn Yard, is seen in the yard at 86C Cardiff (Canton). (A.N.H.Glover)

119) Named after its brilliant designer, LMS *Coronation* Class 4-6-2 No 46256 *Sir William A. Stanier F.R.S.*, allocated to 5A Crewe (North), skirts the shoreline at Penmaenmawr sands, some 229 miles from London (Euston) with a parcels train on 21st August 1964. Constructed at Crewe Works in 1947, No 46256 was the penultimate member of the class. Sadly it was withdrawn less than two months after this picture was taken and scrapped shortly afterwards. (T.R.Amos)

120) Former Great Western tank engine power on show in the shed yard at 86F Tondu during 1954. In the foreground is 4500 Class 2-6-2T No 5556, a local steed which ended its revenue earning days based at 89C Machynlleth in December 1959, being cut up at Swindon Works in early 1960. Lurking in the background is another local engine, GWR 5700 Class 0-6-0PT No 9649 which survived until July 1965, being withdrawn from 86B Newport (Ebbw Junction). (L.Brownhill)

121) The last days of passenger working on the Neath to Pontypool Road line brought all types of locomotives onto the scene, GWR *Grange* and *Hall* Class 4-6-0's, 4300 Class 2-6-0's, LMS Class 8F 2-8-0's and on a dull summer's day in 1963 BR Class 4 2-6-4T No 80133, then allocated to 87A Neath, arrives in the bay platform at Pontypool Road with a train from Neath. Once of the Eastern Region, No 80133 ended its days on the Southern Region. (D.K.Jones)

122) A soaking wet and generally miserable day at Merthyr station on 30th November 1957. As parcels and packages are loaded/unloaded in an adjacent platform, smoke and steam swirl around GWR 6400 Class 0-6-0PT No 6423, a local steed from 88D, as it departs from Merthyr with the 12.46pm for Abergavenny. The 6400 series of tank engines numbered forty in total and No 6423 along with sister engine No 6417 were the first to be withdrawn, in August 1958. (S.L.C.Philips)

123) The original depot at Shrewsbury was opened in 1856 and was the property of the Shrewsbury and Hereford Railway. It ended up as a large affair with three straight shed structures hemming in a covered roundhouse. Parked outside the 'LMS' shed on 9th April 1960 is GWR *Hall* Class 4-6-0 No 4947 *Nanhoran Hall*, from 82B St.Philip's Marsh. This was one of only a handful of *Halls* not to be seen by the author during his many years of trainspotting. (D.K.Jones)

124) Seven months after the inception of British Railways, former Great Central Railway 9F Class LNER N5 Class, 0-6-2T No E9289 is photographed with its footplate crew in the shed yard at the GCR depot at Wrexham (Rhosddu) on 25th July 1948. Owned by the LMR it was coded 6E from 1949-1958 after which it was taken over by the Western Region authorities and coded 84K until closure in April 1960. After this it was used for storage purposes until 1964. (A.N.H.Glover)

125) Its long and industrious career almost over, GWR 2800 Class 2-8-0 No 3855 is photographed in steam by the coaling stage at its home depot at 6C Croes Newydd (Wrexham) on 29th June 1965 in the company of an unidentified member of the BR Class 2 2-6-2 Tanks. Once of 86G Pontypool Road, No 3855 had found its way to Croes Newydd via the sheds at 86C Cardiff (Canton), 84C Banbury and 6E Oswestry. Withdrawn in August 1965 it is now preserved. (Brian Bennett)

126) This quiet setting is a far cry from the days when BR Class 4 2-6-4T No 80096 was allocated to 33A Plaistow and 33B Tilbury and used on heavy local passenger trains to and from London's Fenchurch Street station. In August 1962, no longer required by the Eastern Region authorities, No 80096 was drafted to the Western Region. On 26th July 1963 it is seen at the head of the 'one-coach' 1.30pm departure from Pwllheli station. (H.L.Holland)

127) To the average enthusiast of the late fifties and early sixties it was always most satisfying to see the modern image diesels in trouble and even more satisfying when a steam engine had to render assistance. On 19th May 1963 an unidentified Hymeck diesel-hydraulic has to suffer the humiliation of being 'assisted' into Neath (General) station by GWR 5700 Class 0-6-0PT No 9625 (87A Neath) which proudly displays its 'express' headcode. (D.K.Jones)

128) Located near to the river Cynon the single turntable depot at Aberdare was opened by the GWR in 1908, replacing an older shed. It was situated on the northern side of the Low Level station at Aberdare, a ten minute walk for those on foot. It was coded 86J and 88J under BR and closed completely on 1st March 1965. On 10th May 1962 one of its longstanding inmates, GWR 5700 Class 0-6-0PT No 3699, is seen in the yard. (D.K.Jones)

129) Under the direction of C.B.Collett twenty 2-8-0 Tanks were rebuilt in 1934 into 2-8-2 Tank becoming the 7200 Class. The frames were lengthened rearwards to provide a six-ton capacity bunker and increasing the water capacity to 2,500 gallons. All in all fifty-four engines were eventually rebuilt. On 7th August 1961, No 7222 basks in the warm sunshine in the yard of its home shed at 86A Newport (Ebbw Junction) in the company of 2-8-0T No 5259. (N.E.Preedy)

130) In this next photograph we see one of the earlier GWR 4200 Class 2-8-0 Tanks at work. No 4277, from 86E Severn Tunnel Junction, coasts through Newport (High Street) station on 14th August 1963 with a mixed bag of goods wagons. Unlike No 7222 in the previous picture, No 4277 has inside steampipes and comes from a class of engines originally introduced in 1910. Once of 86H/86F Aberbeeg it was withdrawn from service in June 1964. (B.W.L.Brooksbank)

131) With the fireman standing atop the tender, 84A Wolverhampton (Stafford Road) based GWR *County* Class 4-6-0 No 1016 *County of Hants*, looking in rather less than pristine condition sports express headlamps as it waits near to a boarded crossing at Shrewsbury station in the mid-fifties. Later equipped with a double chimney in March 1957, it spent the last years of its life based at Shrewsbury shed, being condemned from there in September 1963. (D.K.Jones)

132) Quite what GWR 2251 Class 0-6-0 No 3205 was doing at 6G Llandudno Junction in September 1965 and fitted with a snowplough is unknown. What is known is that it had been withdrawn from 83G Templecombe four months earlier and was earmarked for active preservation, firstly on the Severn Valley Railway and in later years on the West Somerset Railway. No 3205 also served from 85A Worcester, 84G Shrewsbury and 89C Machynlleth to mention but a few. (N.L.Browne)

133) Situated on the Aberdare/Merthyr to Cardiff line the small shed at Abercynon (88E) never boasted anything larger than a tank engine on its books. Facing the camera in bright sunshine on 14th October 1962 is locally based GWR 5700 Class 0-6-0PT No 3730 behind which is another local steed GWR 5600 Class 0-6-2T No 5686. Yet another local engine in the frame is sister engine No 5685 flanked by two unidentified 5700 Class 0-6-0 Pannier Tanks. (N.E.Preedy)

134) For those on foot the shed at Cardiff (Canton) was a good ten-minute walk from General station, but once there it was well worth it. A large footbridge spanned the tracks in the yard and also provided access for those brave enough to make the dash over open ground into the shed itself. Standing in the yard on 22nd May 1955 is GWR *Hall* Class 4-6-0 No 4929 *Goytrey Hall*, from 85B Gloucester (Horton Road) which was built in May 1929. (F.Hornby)

135) Double-heading was a common feature during steam days and on 26th April 1958 BR Class 5 4-6-0 No 73132 (84G Shrewsbury) and GWR *Castle* Class 4-6-0 No 5003 *Lulworth Castle*, from 86C Cardiff (Canton), combine to power a West of England express out of Hereford. *Lulworth Castle* was the last of the class to be 'spotted' by the author, at 83A Newton Abbot on 29th April 1962, four months before being withdrawn. No 73132 lived until April 1968. (Denis Lewis)

136) Two months after being transferred from 21D Aston, 6G Llandudno Junction based BR *Britannia* Class 4-6-2 No 70017 *Arrow* steams into Chester (General) station with a Crewe to Llandudno excursion (1D52) on 20th July 1963. Standing next to *Arrow* is an unidentified LMS Class 5 'Caprotti' 4-6-0 with the excursion reporting No 1D57. Before being withdrawn in September 1966 *Arrow* served at both Crewe (North) and South, Newton Heath and Carlisle (Kingmoor) sheds. (D.K.Jones)

137) Although long closed to steam the shed at 87C Danygraig continued to host the odd visitor for a number of years thereafter as can be seen by the presence of 87D Swansea East Dock owned BR Class 4 2-6-4T No 80097 which is standing outside the depot out of steam on 11th November 1962. In common with a large number of members of the same class No 80097 was transferred from the Eastern to the Western Region in the summer of 1962. (N.E.Preedy)

138) The Taff Vale Railway H Class 0-6-0 Tanks were specially designed in 1884 with a sloping firebar crown and tapered boiler for working on the Pwllyrhebog incline, part of which was 1 in 13. It had its own small loco shed at the top of the incline until closure in July 1951. This trio of unique locomotives, GWR Nos. 193-195, spent their entire working lives based at Treherbert shed where they are seen together on 21st July 1951. (T.B.Owen)

139) The last passenger train of the day leaves Moat Lane Junction for the long journey through the Welsh mountains to far-off Brecon via Llanidloes, Builth Road, Three Cocks Junction and Talyllyn Junction (all long closed) at 5.30pm on 14th July 1952. The sparsely patronised three-coach train is in the very capable hands of GWR 'Dean Goods' 0-6-0 No 2409, from a pedigree of 1883, which withdrawn before the fifties came to a close. (Peter Hay)

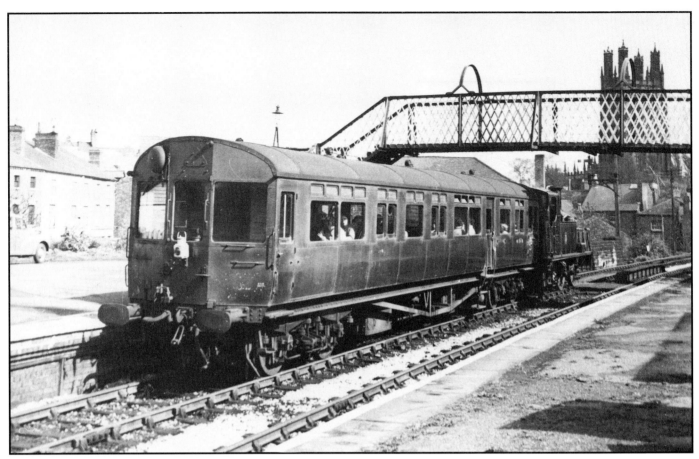

140) GWR 1400 Class 0-6-2T No 1458, from 89D Oswestry, awaits departure from Wrexham (Central) station with an auto-train bound for Ellesmere on a sun-filled day in April 1962. This former Cambrian Railways branch line closed during the same year along with the associated stations at Marchwiel, Pickhill Halt, Bangor-on-Dee, Cloy Halt, Overton-on-Dee, Trench Halt and Elson Halt. No 1458 survived in service until November 1964. (Kit Windle)

141) The roof structure at Shrewsbury station is a shambles on 9th May 1963. On station pilot duty is LMS Class 5 4-6-0 No 45283, a longstanding resident of Shrewsbury shed, which later on in life also served at 6B Mold Junction, 2E Saltley and 2B Oxley prior to condemnation in January 1967. In charge of the 5.33pm local passenger to Ludlow is another local engine BR Class 4 2-6-4T No 80100 (minus front numberplate) which survived until July 1965. (J.Schatz)

142) Situated in between the lines to Newport and Aberdare the depot at Pontypool Road, coded 86G, consisted of a large covered roundhouse and a straight shed. Most of its allocation was freight orientated but it also had some GWR *Grange and Hall* Classes of 4-6-0's on its books prior to complete closure in May 1965. One of its inmates, GWR 6400 Class 0-6-0PT No 6424, still bears the initials of the GWR in the yard at 86G on 15th April 1951. (B.W.L.Brooksbank)

143) Although slightly 'Westernised' the ROD 2-8-0's based on the Western Region are unmistakeably a spin-off from J.G.Robinson's Great Central Railway engines which later became the 04 Class of the LNER. The GWR purchased 100 of them after the First World War though fifty were quickly scrapped. No 3011, from 87G Carmarthen, was one of the lucky survivors and is seen at 87B Duffryn Yard (Port Talbot) on 11th August 1957, a year before withdrawal. (B.K.B.Green)

144) GWR Class 0F 0-4-0ST No 1338 was an 1893 design by Kitson for the Cardiff Railway and with its weight a mere 25 tons 10 cwt., it was an ideal locomotive for negotiating the tightly curved lines in dockyards. Allocated for a number of years at 83B Taunton it was a common sight on shunting duties at Bridgwater. Allocated to 87D Swansea East Dock in June 1960 it is noted in a siding there on 16th September 1962, complete with warning bell. (J.Schatz)

145) Having negotiated the fearsome Severn tunnel, BR Class 5 4-6-0 No 73026 attacks the gradient through Pilning station with the 8.20am express from Manchester to Penzance on 17th June 1961. Allocated to 89A Shrewsbury, No 73026 later worked from the depots at 2L Leamington, 2A Tyseley and 9K Bolton. Withdrawn from the latter in April 1967 it was placed in store for several months before being despatched to Cashmores, Newport. (R.Picton)

146) A large hill in the background dominates the landscape at Penmaenmawr, situated between Conway and Llanfairfechan, as LMS Stanier *Coronation* Class 4-6-2 No 46240 *City of Coventry* from 5A Crewe (North), shows the value of smoke deflectors as it sweeps along the North Wales main line with a lengthy parcels train on 20th August 1964, a few short weeks before being taken out of service. It was scrapped at Cashmores, Great Bridge later in the year. (T.R.Amos)

147) Possibly recently outshopped from Caerphilly Works, GWR 9400 Class 0-6-0PT No 9429, from 85A Worcester, finds itself in bright sunshine outside the running shed at 86C Cardiff (Canton) on 19th June 1960. Briefly based at 85D Bromsgrove from August to September 1961 for use as a banker on the Lickey incline, No 9429 then returned to Worcester shed. Its final home was at 87F Llanelly from March 1962 up to withdrawal in December 1963. (A.N.H.Glover)

148) Designed for express passenger work LMS *Royal Scot* Class 4-6-0 No 46152 *The King's Dragoon Guardsman*, of 6J Holyhead, is relegated to the minor duty of hauling a six-coach local passenger train, seen in a bay platform at Chester prior to setting off eastwards to Crewe. Despite this humiliation *The King's Dragoon Guardsman* was destined to be one of the last active members of the class, being withdrawn from 12A Carlisle (Kingmoor) in 1965. (Kit Windle)

149) For many years an Eastern Region engine at 33A Plaistow and 33B Tilbury, BR Class 4 2-6-4T No 80134 spent exactly two years on the Western Region, being based at 87D Swansea East Dock and 87F Llanelly from August 1962 to August 1964. After this date it was drafted to the Southern Region and worked from the sheds at 70B Feltham and 70F Bournemouth. In this picture it is seen in the shed yard at Swansea East Dock on a September day in 1962. (N.E.Preedy)

150) Looking at this photograph one can understand how labour-intensive the steam locomotive was. Apart from some depots with modern coaling facilities many had to make do with being coaled by hand from small hoppers inside the coal stages. This time-consuming process is being applied to former Taff Vale 0-6-2T No 290 photographed at 88B Cardiff East Dock shed on 3rd October 1954. No 290 had been rebuilt with a taper boiler by the GWR. (W.Potter)

151) 86E Severn Tunnel based GWR 2800 Class 2-8-0 No 3834 trundles past the photographer near to Patchway on 16th March 1960. Between Patchway and Pilning the up and down tracks are independent of one another to allow trains climbing away from the Severn tunnel at an unbroken ascent of 1 in 100 for just over three miles, instead of the changing grades on the down line. No 3834 left 86E for pastures new at 81C Southall in December 1962. (D.K.Jones)

152) The 1101 Class 3F 0-4-0 Tanks were designed by the Avonside Engineering Company for the Great Western Railway and were used primarily for dock shunting. Although first introduced in 1926 the class of six engines were still all at work in January 1957 based at 87C Danygraig. With the introduction of the diesel shunter they were all withdrawn by January 1960. On 1st June 1958, No 1102 is seen at Danygraig in the company of a GWR 5700 Class 0-6-0PT. (N.E.Preedy)

153) Once on the books at 10C Patricroft, LMS Class 2P 4-4-0 No 40635 had been allocated to 6G Llandudno Junction in September 1958. In this portrait it lies rusting on the store line at 6G on 26th August 1962 many months after withdrawal from the shed in February 1961. Because withdrawals in 1961/62 outstripped the capacity to scrap this vast horde of engines, No 40635 was to remain at Llandudno Junction until April 1963. (J.Schatz)

154) Looking fresh from overhaul at Swindon, 88A Cardiff (Canton) based GWR *Manor* Class 4-6-0 No 7805 *Broome Manor* stands at Cardiff (General) station on a frosty but bright 27th December 1961 with an express. *Broome Manor* worked in Wales from Canton and Cardiff East Dock sheds from September 1958 until June 1963, after which it moved to Birmingham at 84E Tyseley. It was condemned in December 1964 and was cut up at Cashmores, Great Bridge. (R.W.Hinton)

155) Under clear signals LMS Class 8F 2-8-0 No 48083, from 17A Derby, reverses through Shrewsbury station which is obviously being rebuilt judging by the amount of rubble on the platform in the left of this picture on 16th June 1962. A few months before Derby shed closed to steam, No 48083 was moved to 16G Westhouses in September 1966. One month later and it was on the move again, this time to 16B Colwick where it died a month later. (D.K.Jones)

156) Passengers and station staff mingle together near to the station canopy adjoining the main station building at Ellesmere in March 1957. In charge of a local passenger working is 89C Machynlleth allocated GWR 'Dukedog' Class 2P 4-4-0 No 9004. Four months on and No 9004 was at a new and final home at 84J Croes Newydd, being withdrawn in June 1960. Ellesmere station on the lines from Wrexham, and Oswestry to Whitchurch closed in 1965. (N.E.Preedy)

157) GWR 5700 Class 0-6-0PT No 3731 is a visitor to 88J Aberdare from 87A Neath on a summer's day in 1962. A longstanding inmate of 82B St.Philip's Marsh in Bristol, No 3731 had been transferred to 83E St.Blazey in deepest Cornwall in September 1961. Upon the closure of St.Blazey to steam at the end of April 1962 it was drafted to South Wales at Neath shed. Condemned in May 1964 it was despatched to Birds, Bynea for scrapping two months later. (D.K.Jones)

158) With the footplate crew hiding within the warmth of the cab of their charge, GWR 9400 Class 0-6-0PT No 9442, newly transferred to 88C Barry from 87B Duffryn Yard and looking fresh from overhaul, canters through Cardiff (General) with a goods train in October 1962. The stay at Barry shed was shortlived for No 9442 for it was moved on to 87A Neath the following month. Condemnation and oblivion for No 9442 came in July 1964. (D.K.Jones)

159) Minus shedplate and sporting a triangular plate with 'H AUTO 1' on the bufferbeam which is partially covered in ash is locally based GWR 6400 Class 0-6-0PT No 6435 seen in the yard of its home shed at 88A Cardiff (Cathays) on 14th August 1953. Transferred to 88E Abercynon in November 1957, No 6435 remained there until August 1962. It was withdrawn from Yeovil shed in October 1964 and has since been preserved on the Dart Valley Railway. (D.K.Jones)

160) Constructed at Swindon Works in November 1949, GWR 5101 Class 2-6-2T No 4177 poses for the camera in the shed yard at 88C Barry on 22nd May 1955. Allocated to 88A Cardiff (Cathays) it was ousted from the latter in December 1957 when it became a sub-shed, moving on to the depot at Radyr, newly coded 88A. It was destined to remain in active service at Radyr until withdrawn in May 1965. Birds, Bridgend cut it up three months later. (F.Hornby)

161) Amongst the network of lines in the Cardiff area was the small branch to Riverside and Clarence Road stations, both of which closed in 1964. Sporting express headlamps GWR 9400 Class 0-6-0PT No 8464, from 86C Cardiff (Canton), is photographed at Riverside station on 3rd June 1958. In November 1959, No 8464 found a new home at 84B Oxley. Between then and withdrawal in December 1963 it also worked from 81A Old Oak Common and 81D Reading. (D.K.Jones)

162) A gaggle of spotters occupy the end of one of the platforms at Chester station and jot down the number of GWR *Grange* Class 4-6-0 No 6867 *Peterston Grange*, of far-off 87A Neath, as it enters with a lengthy parcels train on 20th July 1963. *Peterston Grange* had been based in Wales since May 1958, firstly at 86G Pontypool Road and then Neath (June 1963). It remained in Wales until being condemned from 87F Llanelly in August 1964. (D.K.Jones)

163) Two 89C Machynlleth based locomotives, BR Class 2 2-6-0 No 78007 and BR Class 3 2-6-2T No 82033, combine together to head a Pwllheli to Birmingham (Snow Hill) express at Barmouth station on 30th June 1962. The fortunes of both of these engines varied with No 82033 surviving until September 1965 after spells at 6H Bangor and 70A Nine Elms. No 78007 remained in service until January 1967 with 9K Bolton being its final abode. (B.W.L.Brooksbank)

164) A trio of GWR *Castle* Class 4-6-0's are lined up outside the running shed at 87E Landore (Swansea) in the late fifties. From left to right are Nos 5030 *Shirburn Castle*, from 87G Carmarthen, 7002 *Devizes Castle*, a local engine, and 4082 *Windsor Castle*, of 81A Old Oak Common. *Shirburn Castle* was the first to be withdrawn, from 87G in September 1962, followed by *Devizes Castle* in March 1964. *Windsor Castle* survived until September 1964. (Denis Lewis)

165) Despite the fact that it is many years after nationalisation GWR 5700 Class 0-6-0PT No 7712 is still carrying the initials of its former owner in the shed yard at 86B Newport (Pill) on 14th September 1952. Once owned by the Alexandra Docks Railway, Newport (Pill) was opened in 1875 and it consisted of a lengthy twin track running shed structure with extensive sidings in the yard to house its allocation. It closed in June 1963. (N.E.Preedy

166) Bright sunshine and dark shadows at Cardiff (Riverside) station where the suspended clock informs us that it is almost ten minutes to one in the afternoon. The station is almost deserted as we espy GWR 6400 Class 0-6-0PT No 6438, of 88E Abercynon, which is in charge of a Clarence Road to Pontypridd local passenger train on 2nd May 1959. No 6438 ended its days operating from 83D Laira (Plymouth), being condemned in November 1962. (S.L.C.Philips)

167) GWR *County* Class 4-6-0 No 1003 *County of Wilts*, locally based at 84G, pilots an unidentified GWR 4-6-0 with a heavy express as they both arrive at Shrewsbury station on an unknown date in 1955. Equipped with a double chimney in November 1957, *County of Wilts* was reallocated to 83D Laira (Plymouth) in January 1961. Withdrawn from Laira in October 1962, No 1003 was stored there until being despatched for scrapping in January 1964. (D.K.Jones)

168) Twin plumes of white smoke merge together as LMS Webb Coal Tank 0-6-2T No 58926, from 84G Shrewsbury, and former London and North Western Railway Class 7F 0-8-0 No 49121, based at 86K Tredegar, combine to head the last train from Merthyr to Abergavenny on 5th January 1958, which is about to enter Clydach tunnel. Both engines were withdrawn during the same year, 1958, No 49121 from 86K in September and No 58926 from 86G Pontypool Road in November. (S.L.C.Philips)

169) Collett GWR 6400 Class 0-6-0PT No 6424 (built at Swindon in 1935) is seen in the yard at 88C Barry on 19th June 1949 still bearing the initials GWR. These engines were a development of Dean's 2021 Class of 1897 and with the similar 5400 series were built as replacements as the older engines became worn out. They were used mainly on one or two coach auto-trains on steeply graded branch lines in South Wales and the Black Country of England. (A.N.H.Glover)

170) It is almost the end of the road for GWR 2251 Class 0-6-0 No 2271, from 89C Machynlleth, as it stands in a line of locomotives in the shed yard at 89B Croes Newydd on 2nd September 1962. Based at Machynlleth during the latter part of the fifties, No 2271 worked from 87H Neyland from May to September 1958 before moving on to 87J Goodwick until July 1962. Condemned from 89C in September 1962 it was eventually scrapped at Hayes, Bridgend in 1963. (J.Schatz)

171) No photograph album devoted to Wales would be complete without a visit to the once infamous Barry Docks scrapyard where countless locomotives were cut up over the years. On Monday 7th April 1969 condemned and rotting steam engines are lined up in rows as far as the eye can see. All looks lost in this sad picture, but as the saying goes 'hope springs eternal' and a great many of the locomotives seen here have been saved for posterity. (A.C.Ingram)

172) Having just stated the latter we move on to 1975 and the preservation movement associated with Barry Docks is gathering momentum. After years of being exposed to the sea air GWR *Hall* Class 4-6-0 No 4920 *Dumbleton Hall* has been sold to the Dart Valley Railway, departing from Barry in June 1976. Withdrawn from 81F Oxford in December 1965, *Dumbleton Hall* had been in store at Barry since February 1966. Also in the frame are two BR Class 4 2-6-4 Tanks. (D.K.Jones)